GRE[illegible]
AND TRAGEDY

ποῦ μοι τὰ ῥόδα, ποῦ μοι τὰ ἴα, ποῦ μοι τὰ καλὰ σέλινα;
"ταδὶ τὰ ῥόδα, ταδὶ τὰ ἴα, ταδὶ τὰ καλὰ σέλινα."

Where are my roses? Where are my violets?
Where are my pretty garlands?
"Here are my roses! Here are my violets!
Here are my pretty garlands!"

FOLK-SONG

GREEK LYRIC POETRY AND TRAGEDY

TRANSLATION AND
ORIGINAL COMPOSITION
BY
EREZ NATANBLUT

Laodamia Press
Dedicated to Ancient Greek Poetry and Drama

Montreal, 2005

Published by **LAODAMIA PRESS**, Montreal, Quebec, Canada

Typography and Cover Design by Joel Natanblut

Laodamia Press
Dedicated to Ancient Greek Poetry and Drama

Printed and bound in Canada

Library and Archives Canada Cataloguing in Publication

Greek lyric poetry and tragedy / translation and original composition by Erez Natanblut.

Also available on Audiobook CD.

ISBN 0-9739026-0-4

1. Greek poetry--Translations into English. I. Natanblut, Erez, 1968-

PA3621.G74 2005 884′.01 C2005-905345-3

CONTENTS

GREEK LYRIC POETRY

GREEK TRAGEDY

GREEK LYRIC POETRY

θεὸς ὁ τὰ πάντα τεύχων βροτοῖς

καὶ χάριν ἀοιδᾷ φυτεύει.

God, the fashioner of all things for mortals,

also creates the gracefulness in melody.

PINDAR

ἀνδρῶν δικαίων χρόνος σωτὴρ ἄριστος.

Time is the sole saviour of the just.

PINDAR

EREZ NATANBLUT

SONNET TO THE LABYRINTH

Wintry Labyrinth,
keeper of the yelping Minotaur,
your walls are made
not of stone,
but of smoldering ice,
which neither a sledgehammer
nor axe
can wedge a crack.
In your corridors
gusty winds howl,
refrigerating the air,
while snowflakes dive down,
glittering like the heavenly stars.
In you roams the Minotaur,
frightened and bewildered
without his beloved Ariadne,
who visits daily,
bringing him food, cotton socks,
woolen sweaters, and new thermal boots,
if need be.
Often she'll pick up his book
lying open on the ground,
its pages bent
and covered by snow
yearning to be words.

SAPPHO

HELP ME, APHRODITE

Immortal Aphrodite of the galvanized Throne,
Daughter of Zeus and weaver of Mischief,
Don't make my Heart grieve and groan,
   My dear Lady;

But come to me as before,
When my voice shot through your door
And you left your father's
   Golden Palace.

You yoked your chariot to Sparrows,
Whose wings became soaked in the Wind's marrows,
As they soared over the dark earth from
   Heaven to Sky.

You arrived quickly
And smiled blissfully,
Asking what ails me,
   Why I call,

And why I now rage:
"Whom should Love's persuasion encage
And who is bad
   To you, Sappho?

If she flees, soon she'll cling;
If she accepts no gifts, soon many she'll fling;
If she's repulsed, soon she'll love
   Against her will."

Come to me now,
Unleash my Cares,
And glut my Desires
   As my Ally.

LOVE'S POWER

That man is a god,
who sits beside you, woman,
and hears your
   sensuous

talk and luscious laugh,
a sight that pounds my heart.
When I look at you,
   I can't talk,

my tongue becomes numb,
flames down my legs hum,
my eyes blur, and whispers blare
   in my ears.

Sweat anoints my skin,
trembling comes over me with a din,
and, like parched grass, I'm
   half alive.

A GARDEN

Here the apple trees mutter
To the cold river water,
While roses perfume the air
And dreams linger on leaves without care.

SLEEP

The moon is translucent,
and so are the Pleiades.
It's the middle of night,
and I sleep
alone.

HER BEAUTY

Stars, the moon's neighbours,
illuminate her voluptuous figure
upon the whole earth.

NIGHTINGALE

The honey-tongued nightingale
is spring's messenger.

HYACINTH

On the hills shepherds trample over the hyacinth,
and purple is spread on the ground.

A WOMAN

Like when a sweet apple blushes
on the top branch,
the top of the highest branch.
The apple pickers forgot it.
No, they didn't:
they couldn't reach it.

DEATH

When you die,
no one will remember
or desire you;
nor will you inhale the roses
of Pieria.
But invisible
in the house of Hades,
you'll flutter
among shady corpses.

SIMONIDES

DANAE AND PERSEUS

When in the carved chest
the wind stirred,
the sea stood still,
and tears ran down her cheeks,
she tucked baby Perseus
under the sheets and said:
"Such troubles I have,
while you slumber
carefree
on a plank bed that's shaded
by the blue night.
You pay no attention to the waves
or wind's roar,
but simply rest your head
on a woolen pillow.
If you knew what danger is
you'd not let my words flit and miss.
Sleep, baby, sleep.
May the sea sleep,
and may our misery sleep.
Father Zeus,
save us
and forgive me,
if I ever uttered a boastful
or wrongful word."

ORPHEUS

Birds flew over his head,
and fish somersaulted out of the water,
all applauding his delectable rhythms.

IBYCUS

EROS

It is in spring
when the Kydonian apple trees
drink from the streams,
which also water the maidens' sacred garden
and vines that offer green shade
to the sky.
Yet for me
never rests Eros,
who, like Thracian Boreas,
blazes with lightning from Aphrodite's house,
jealous, furious, fearless,
and ready to uproot my heart
from the ground.

ARCHILOCHUS

MY GIRLFRIEND

Lovingly she holds myrtle
   and booming roses,
while her hair droops
   upon her shoulders
and back.

MY SPEAR

On my spear you'll find
   a loaf of bread.
On my spear you'll find
   some vintage wine.
Leaning on my spear,
   I imbibe.

PINDAR

WINE IS AN OCEAN

When anxiety is unburdened,
we swim in wealth's golden ocean
towards an imaginary shore.
The poor become rich
and the rich become wiser,
pierced by vine arrows.

ALCMAN

MOUNT RHIPA

Mount Rhipa,
the forest blossom,
is the chest
of black night.

CALLIOPE

Hey Muse,
Calliope,
Zeus' daughter,
begin your lovely song
that infatuates
and exuberates
the gratifying dance.

DEW

All these things are nourished by
Dew, the daughter of Zeus and Selene.

BIRDS

I know the note of every bird.

LYRE

The lyre competes with iron.

SLEEP

Sleep soothes the mountaintops, crags,
headlands, ravines,
beasts that are fed by the black earth,
and fish that drink the ocean's belly.
Sleep also soothes the race
of feathered birds.

PHRYNICHUS

LOVE'S RAYS

Love's rays radiate
violet cheeks.

MIMNERMUS

OLD AGE

What life, what pleasures are without golden Aphrodite?
   May I die, when I no longer care for
secret love, fine gifts, and marriage -
   the tender flowers of youth
for men and women. When grievous old age arrives
   - the disgraceful bane -
sorrows diminish his heart;
   he doesn't enjoy looking at the sun
and is abominable to children and
   unattractive to women.
So has god made old age difficult.

HELIOS

The Sun has daily toils
   and, like his horses, never rests
after rosy-fingered Dawn leaves Ocean
   and enters Heaven.
Carried over the waves by his comfy air-bed
   that has been crafted by Hephaestus
with precious gold, the Sun skims over the water
   from the land of Hesperides
to the land of the Ethiopians,
   where his swift chariot and horses await
Dawn's arrival.
   Here the son of Hyperion sets off.

STESICHORUS

HELEN

The story isn't true;
you didn't sail in those ships,
nor did you ever go to Troy.

GOLDEN CUP

The Sun steps into his golden cup,
  which torpedoes him through the black night
to his mother, wife, and children.
  He then enters the laurel grove.

XENOPHANES
SYMPOSIUM

Here the floors, cups,
   and hands are clean.
Some people crown their heads with leaves,
   while others pass around bottles of perfume.
The carafe is full of cheer,
   offering perfect wine
that's sweet and floral.
   In the middle of the room you'll find
incense exhaling savoury smoke
   and water that's chilly, transparent, and tasty.
On the old table there's golden-crusted bread,
   cheese, and rich honey.
The altar is decorated with flowers,
   and singing permeates the air.
Here we must sing of the gods
   with reverence,
pour libations, and pray to be humble.
   No hubris allowed, please.
Drink as much as you can,
   but, unless you're elderly,
you won't get escorted home.
   I praise the drinker who remains
sensible- the only way to be known
   for character and virtue.
I won't talk about the battles of the Titans,
   Giants, and Centaurs, or the strife
among the gods – the fiction of our ancestors.
   No good will come of this.
Always worship the gods.

< ᾿Αίδας>

< ὃς> μόνος οὐ δέχεται γλυκερᾶς μέρος ἐλπίδος.

Hades is the only one who doesn't receive a share of sweet hope.

ANONYMOUS

LAODAMIA AND STHENEBOEA,

TWO GREEK TRAGEDIES

BY

EREZ NATANBLUT

Laodamia and Stheneboea are reconstructions of two lost plays by Euripides, the Greek tragedian of the fifth century B.C. Meager, tantalizing fragments and ancient plot summaries provided the inspiration for these modern dramatizations of ancient Greek myths.

CHARACTERS

Laodamia	Wife of Protesilaus, the first Greek killed at Troy
Hecate	Goddess of witchcraft
Persephone	Goddess and Queen of the Underworld; wife of Hades
Erictho	Goddess of witchcraft

LAODAMIA

PART ONE

The underworld. Enter Hecate, the goddess of witchcraft, and Laodamia, the wife of Protesilaus.

Hecate This is the underworld,
a cobweb
on which the dead are cocooned.
If you wanted to measure this web,
you'd find it difficult,
for it is boundless,
timeless.
But have no fear:
because I'm a goddess
and you're no shadow,
we'll easily glide over it,
like a pair of doves
playing in the meadow.

Laodamia You're my guide and protector, Hecate,
but I shudder at the dusk,
which pervades with an aura
that's strange and stringent
to my senses.
Is that the river Styx?

Hecate Yes, Laodamia.

Laodamia I've never seen water
whose skin is slippery,
ruby black.
And look at those trees,
drenched with eeriness
and waving to nobody.

Hecate Those are cypresses, sacred to Persephone.

Laodamia I hope Persephone will let my husband leave the underworld. You know, his death was so untimely. Did he have to be killed the moment he stepped off his ship?

Hecate It was his destiny; the oracle even predicted it.

Laodamia The oracle only predicted the death of the first Greek touching Trojan land. It didn't name anyone.

Hecate It didn't have to. But your husband was that first Greek. He shouldn't have disregarded the oracle.

Laodamia He didn't believe in oracles; if he did, he'd be alive now and we wouldn't be here.

Hecate Let's not dwell on this. What's important is we've come to fetch him.

Laodamia I'm nervous. I know I've asked you before, but do you think we'll convince Persephone?

Hecate I do. When she arrives, we'll become Orpheus, enchanting her with sweet, riveting words.

Laodamia Do you think Orpheus is an appropriate model? He failed to save his wife Eurydice.

Hecate I'll make sure we won't fail by any technicality, like he did. We'll follow all of Persephone's instructions if she agrees to restore your husband.

Laodamia Your determination is comforting. By the way, Hecate, how should I act before her? Should I address her in a regal way?

Hecate No, be natural and direct. *(pauses; her voice suddenly becomes timid)* It's been a while since I've been in the underworld. You know, I once used to live here; that was before I went to

Mount Olympus.

Laodamia I didn't know you lived in the underworld; I thought Mount Olympus was always your home. Why did you leave? Did you find this place depressing and dreary?

Hecate No.

Laodamia What was the reason?

Hecate Because I quarreled with Persephone. I haven't talked to her since.

Laodamia If you don't mind me asking, what was the quarrel about?

Hecate Persephone accused me of gossiping. This, of course, was untrue. I denied the charge, but she didn't believe me. Our relationship then changed. She became cold and distant, and so did her husband. It became so unbearable that I had to vacate these premises and go to Mount Olympus.

Laodamia If I knew about this, I wouldn't have accepted your help. I don't want you to be put in an awkward situation.

Hecate Don't worry about my awkwardness; I'll deal with it as it arises. Besides, I'm kind of excited being here. The underworld was my first home.

Laodamia Helping me then was an excuse to return.

Hecate Partly, but I couldn't stand on Mount Olympus and watch you take your own life, my friend.

Laodamia That was a difficult period, when I found out about my husband's death. Life without him is unbearable, unimaginable; and the first road I attempted to tread was suicide. But you appeared, dissuading me from self-destruction and promising a hopeful outcome from this journey. Doubts, however, still linger in me.

Hecate Don't have doubts; this will only bring failure. Laodamia - to show you the extent of my conviction and the belief of our cause - I'm even willing to confront my archrival.

Laodamia Who's your archrival?

Hecate Erictho, the other goddess of witchcraft.

Laodamia I didn't know there was another witch-goddess besides you.

Hecate *(emotionally)* Erictho too has the power to boil the sea, tumble the earth, and liquefy the sky. I believe she caused the quarrel between Persephone and me.

Laodamia That's terrible. I hope we can avoid Erictho and deal only with Persephone. Were you and Persephone close friends?

Hecate We were. I was her first friend in the underworld. But it'll be difficult to avoid Erictho; she has immense influence over Persephone and easily sways her mind. I hope my old friendship will overcome any obstacles Erictho may throw before us. Being here, however, brings back fond memories; life in the underworld wasn't always unpleasant.

Laodamia Do you know where can we find Persephone? I'm anxious.

Hecate She'll find us. That's her throne. *(pointing)* She always knows when somebody is waiting for her.

PART TWO

Persephone enters. She is surprised to see Hecate, whom she addresses indifferently.

Persephone Hecate.

Hecate Persephone.

Persephone It's been a while.

Hecate It has.

Persephone What brings you to my humble abode? I'm surprised to see you; you said you'd never return.

Hecate I did say that, but time has soothed my anger. I've returned on a mission.

Persephone What's your mission? And why have you brought this woman? You know the rules: it's forbidden for the living to enter these precincts.

Hecate I know it's forbidden, but I'm breaking the rules for a good reason. She's Laodamia. Perhaps you know her husband; he recently died at Troy.

Persephone What's his name?

Hecate Protesilaus.

Persephone I don't think I know him. It's hard for me to keep track of all our residents, including new arrivals.

Hecate He's quite famous. He was the first Greek to die at Troy.

Persephone How did he die?

Hecate He was killed upon touching Trojan land.

Persephone Oh yes, I remember. My husband Hades talked about him the other day. *(turning to Laodamia)*

Did you come to visit your husband's ghost?

Laodamia Yes and no.

Persephone What do you mean?

Laodamia I've come to fetch him, with your permission of course.

Persephone *(authoritatively)* I don't know what Hecate has told you, but it's forbidden to make the dead alive.

Laodamia Hecate told me you have the power.

Hecate Everyone knows about Orpheus.

Persephone We weren't in our right senses when we granted his request; it was his music that drugged us. Otherwise, we wouldn't have agreed.

Laodamia I appeal to you as a wife. You, too, have a husband and can sympathize with my plight. How would you feel if your husband suddenly disappeared, never to be seen or heard again?

Persephone That could never happen: he's immortal, like I am.

Laodamia For argument's sake, let's imagine it happened. Wouldn't you be devastated?

Persephone I guess I would.

Hecate And if you were mortal, wouldn't you have suicidal thoughts, so you could join him?

Persephone Perhaps, if despair overtook me.

Hecate Well, all of this happened to Laodamia. Her life had no meaning after her husband's death. She even attempted suicide, but I saved her. I gave her hope and renewed her will to live.

Persephone You gave her false hope: her husband can't leave.

A kommos (lyric dialogue) begins.

Hecate	You're acquainted with despair. Don't you remember your abduction?
Laodamia	Is the story true?
Persephone	Yes. I was playing in the fields and gathering flowers, when the ground ripped open.
Hecate	Hades leapt out, crazed.
Laodamia	Couldn't you escape?
Persephone	Fear froze me, riveting my legs into the ground.
Hecate	You were then submerged.
Laodamia	It must have been terrifying.
Persephone	It was.
Hecate	And the wedding ceremony was horrific.
Laodamia	How?
Persephone	The torch coughed, the guests were morbid,
Hecate	And the bride was unwilling.
Laodamia	How did you survive?
Persephone	With the help of Hecate, my comforter and saviour.
Hecate	I ended your fast with ambrosia and nectar.
Laodamia	A bond held you both.
Persephone	We were inseparable at all times.
Hecate	You always asked for me.
Laodamia	What ripped your bond?
Persephone	Petty matters interspersed, destroying our friendship.
Hecate	Those petty matters came from Erictho.
Laodamia	Her name resounds with dread.
Persephone	Hecate, you said time has soothed your anger, but the mention of Erictho shows your anger remains solid like ice.

Hecate I'm only stating a fact.

The kommos ends.

Persephone The remembrance of past despair makes me sympathetic and ready to disregard the prohibited. Laodamia, I give you permission to take your husband, but this has to be kept secret. Nobody, including my husband, is to know. Protesilaus is granted a second span of life and will reach old age with you. Now go tell him the good news.

Laodamia Thank you, Persephone. I'm so ecstatic.

Hecate You did the right thing, Persephone.

Laodamia Where can I find him?

Persephone Go down that path, which leads to the Elysian fields. Protesilaus is there with the rest of his companions. Talk to him alone, apart from everyone.

Laodamia exits, running joyfully down the path.

Persephone I'm happy to see you.

Hecate Being here brings back pleasant memories.

Persephone You were once my anchor of sanity.

Hecate It's unfortunate how quarrels end friendships.

PART THREE

Erictho runs in, out of breath. She is agitated and not pleased to see Hecate.

Erictho Persephone, don't agree to her demands! If you've already said yes, say no. *(turning to Hecate)* Hecate, what you want shouldn't be allowed.

Hecate Erictho, hello to you, too. Glad to see you've not changed: you're ready to give orders the moment you arrive. Besides, how do you know what's going on? Were you spying?

Erictho Besides witchcraft, prophecy is another of my specialties. I knew you'd be arriving with a guest by the name of Laodamia. I even knew the purpose of your visit.

Persephone You always amaze me, Erictho.

Hecate There's nothing amazing about her prophetic powers. Aren't there other gods of divination?

Persephone Of course there are. You sound jealous, Hecate.

Hecate I'm not. I'm just astonished at the hold she still has over you.

Persephone She has no special hold over me. Erictho, I've already said yes to Laodamia. I know it's forbidden, but I took pity. We all agreed to keep it hush.

Erictho You have no idea of the havoc you'll be causing. Do you really believe you can keep it hush? No. It'll become public knowledge, and before you know it, every god or goddess will come down and ask you to release a favourite. You'll be bombarded with such requests everyday, every minute. You'll never have a moment's peace. Chaos will reign. Is it really worth releasing Protesilaus? My instincts also tell me that extending people's lives will have ill effects in the cosmos: life and death will become intermeshed without division. Persephone, you have to think about all these consequences. I know you pity Laodamia, but her case is not unique. Many people lose loved ones, but they go on living. This is the lot of human beings.

Hecate What you're saying is preposterous, Erictho. Releasing Protesilaus from the underworld won't be a bad precedent. If a god or goddess happens to find out and asks for the same favour, then refuse, saying that this can't be done anymore. You really don't have anything to fear. And also, extending this man's life won't cause any cosmic upheaval. We're not making him immortal, but only reassigning the date of his death. I promise you, no blurring of life and death will occur in his case or another.

Persephone Erictho, if I refuse Laodamia now, she'll think I'm weak.

Hecate Don't undo what you've done. Stand firm with your decision, Persephone.

Erictho Persephone, you won't look weak if you change your mind. Just explain you acted prematurely, without thinking through the whole matter. You can also blame everything on Hades. Say you asked him and he said no. What he says goes and you can't fight him. It's that easy.

Hecate Persephone, you know you can't lie.

Persephone I'm starting to be troubled by what Erictho said. Chaos might really be unleashed if Protesilaus is brought back to life; and despite our efforts, there's a good chance his release will become public. The idea of daily guests terrifies me; I'll never have peace or quiet. I think I made a mistake. When Laodamia returns, I'll have to tell her she can't leave with her husband. But I won't blame this on Hades. I'll be honest and tell her the truth. Hecate's right. I'm not a good liar.

Erictho Yes! The truth will set you free! If Laodamia can't accept your new decision, so be it.

Hecate Persephone, you promised.

Persephone I know, but I'm afraid of the consequences.

Erictho Hecate, it's best you lay off. You've always been trouble.

Hecate What do you mean by that?

Erictho I don't believe you returned purely on a humanitarian mission. I think you had ulterior motives.

Hecate Such as?

Erictho Finding new gossip about Persephone. You're an expert in that field.

Hecate I find your accusations revolting. I've never spread malicious lies about Persephone, nor have I returned to find new gossip. Did you know, till this day, I'm ignorant of the details contained in the old gossip? I think it's time for me to know.

Persephone Hecate, let's not excavate into the past. I don't remember details.

Hecate I don't believe you. I need to know. *(Sarcastically)*

Maybe I'm a kind of goddess who is careless with words and slanders unawares.

Persephone *(a little agitated)* Let's change subjects.

Hecate *(firmly)* No. I demand to know.

Erictho I'll tell you, Hecate, since you're so anxious.

Persephone Don't.

Erictho And why not? It's time she discovered the impact of her words. *(turning to Hecate)* Did you ever talk to anyone about Persephone's marriage?

Hecate Not beyond the house.

Erictho Well, word went around that Persephone was in a destructive relationship and that this piece of information came from you. This news was heard everywhere - the heavens, the earth, the sea, the underworld - and it made Persephone very upset and angry.

Hecate Persephone, I swear - I never said you were in a destructive relationship. I'm really surprised that you, of all goddesses, believed I was the author of such gossip.

Persephone I did then, but not anymore.

Hecate I always kept your personal life private. I never told anyone about your depression or constant desire to return to your mother.

Erictho Then why was your name always mentioned?

Hecate I don't know. I was obviously framed. *(pauses)* It was probably by you.

Erictho That's preposterous.

Hecate No, it isn't. You had good reason to slander me.

Erictho And what was that?

Hecate You wanted to gain control over Persephone,

	but in order to do this, you had to alienate her from me. And so you started the rumour and blamed it on me. How's that?
Erictho	*(turning to Persephone)* This is outrageous! I hope you don't believe her.
Persephone	This is getting out of hand. Control yourselves. *(steps in between Erictho and Hecate)* This gossip means nothing to me now. I'm more mature and see how it wasn't worth the aggravation it once caused. And I also don't care who started it. My present concern is Laodamia. She's returned. I recognize her footsteps.

PART FOUR

Laodamia enters, exalted. Persephone, Hecate, and even Erictho are uncomfortable.

Laodamia	I'm so excited and happy. I had a wonderful conversation with my husband, and yet it was so strange to see him; if you think about it, it's quite unusual to talk to a ghost. But he won't be a ghost much longer. Soon he'll be reborn, alive again, and we'll leave. Why are you all so quiet? Did I interrupt something? *(notices Erictho)* Are you a goddess, too?
Erictho	Yes. My name is Erictho.
Laodamia	Hecate mentioned your name earlier. I'm Laodamia.
Erictho	I know.
Laodamia	Protesilaus is very excited about leaving. He said it was foolish for having hurried to his death. I guess somebody had to fulfill the

oracle; if it weren't him it would have been another. Yet this doesn't matter anymore. I have him back! Persephone, when can we leave?

Persephone We have to talk.

Laodamia About what? I hope there's no delay.

Persephone It's more than a delay. *(pauses)* Your husband can't leave after all. He has to stay.

Laodamia But you promised. What made you change your mind?

Persephone All I'll say is that there's a reason why we don't raise the dead. If we did, there would be turmoil. I was wrong to think that the rules could be broken.

Laodamia Hecate, can't you do something?

Hecate No, it's beyond my control. You can thank Erictho for the setback.

Laodamia *(looks at Erictho)* Really? *(turning to Persephone)* I don't know what happened during my brief absence, but I beg you to release my husband.

Persephone I'm sorry; I can't.

Laodamia You're a cruel goddess. You shouldn't have led me on; you should have said no at the beginning.

Persephone I didn't mean to be inconsiderate.

Laodamia Hecate, why did we make this journey? To be promised and then refused? What am I going to do? I always had doubts about our success. Despair runs through my whole body.

Persephone This might not be comforting, but I want you to know I commend you for undertaking this journey. Only few of the living have journeyed to dead man's land. Consider yourself privileged. When you return to the land above, report what you've seen here and remind everyone that life is precious and short; enjoy living while you're alive.

Laodamia is visibly distraught.

Hecate *(comfortingly)* Laodamia, I'm at your side.

Choral ode begins.

Laodamia For a brief moment
his demise was of no consequence,
but now it is bewildering,
filling me with sadness
and grief.
I can only think of the tumultuous wave
that rose over his ship
and dashed itself on the prow.
The sail ripped
and jagged weapons jostled
in jittering movement.
Yet fear wasn't in Protesilaus' heart:
he became hungrier for battle,
and when the ship reached shore,
he bounced off
and poured forth
a pool of blood.

Hecate Protesilaus,
you were the eye of the army,
commander on land and sea,
but now you're nothing;
you know nothing.

People spend years perfecting themselves
with study, art, and exercise,
but when a person dies,
knowledge and ability evaporate
without murmur or sound.

Erictho Revulsion is the river
from which shadows drink,
as they stand on the banks,
quivering and quaking.
Delusion is their meal,
and when they gaze
upon the water,
they emit cries of horror
at the hundred suns
and the elastic snakes
weaving and unweaving
their ungodly tapestry.
Fools:
venom isn't demolishment
for the dead,
but their nourishment.

Persephone A spider's web is a trampoline.
Leaves bounce upon it,
and so do embalmed meals.
Violent winds test its flexibility
and prove its durability.
But don't think that the spider
is only an acrobat:
it's also a prophet
who reads the chronicles
of people's lives.
In the underworld
I'm the spider

embroiled in embroidery
and bombarded by souls' history,
past, present, and future.

Laodamia Have you no compunction, Persephone?
I'm a crocus
slaughtered by the plough,
and my future is desolation,
isolation.
Better to have been refused
than raised
and dashed to the ground.
Yet I'm powerless:
can a mortal conquer an immortal?

Hecate I'm the subject of disappointment, too.
I once swore never to return,
but your plight required
my oath's annulment.
I then hoped for reconciliation
and obliteration
of a quarrel I never aspired to,
nor comprehended;
but defeat prevents migration.
Laodamia,
I believed we'd be successful,
relying on integrity
and persuasion;
but the meddling of a rival
upset our plans and wishes.

Erictho All witches worship me supreme
and bow before my majesty.
Go to the moon
and she'll tell you
how I once pulled her down from heaven

and made her prisoner,
so that one night
would last a hundred nights.
Many learn too late
that I'm irresistible,
unconquerable.

Persephone Laodamia, Erictho's boast is not insubstantial:
her beauty is legendary
and her eminence is confirmed
by privilege
and preference.
Do you see the cypress at your right?
That's Erictho's tree,
a secret gateway to Tartarus,
and by its trunk,
she enters underworld's lowest,
unseen and unheard;
but to everyone else
this highway is restricted,
prohibited.

Choral ode ends.

Laodamia Who's going to tell my husband the bad news? I can't.

Persephone I'll go since I'm responsible for the change in plans. But I don't want to go alone. Hecate, do you mind coming along?

Hecate *(nods reluctantly)*

Erictho What about me?

Persephone You may come, too. Laodamia, we'll return shortly.

Persephone, Hecate, and Erictho depart. Laodamia sits on the ground, holding her head in her hands.

PART FIVE

Erictho returns, holding a box in her hands. She places it on the table. Laodamia looks up at Erictho and is surprised at her quick return; however, she pays no attention to the box.

Laodamia You've returned quickly.

Erictho I left the other two with your husband. Persephone sent me back; she thought it'd be better if I kept you company until they return. It's taking longer than thought.

Laodamia Why?

Erictho Protesilaus is upset and arguing with them. He feels cheated.

Laodamia As I do. Do you think he can convince Persephone?

Erictho No more than you did. By the way, how are you holding up?

Laodamia Not very well. I was reluctant to make this trip, but Hecate convinced me. You know, it's strange, I always knew I'd make this journey.

Erictho How is that?

Laodamia From a dream I had a long time ago.
(stands up)
I dreamt I stood on a hill,
overlooking a city below.
The grey walls shivered in the dancing dust,
the houses bent sideways,
and out of the square windows
crept

rays of darkness.
I wasn't alone, but with friends,
and turning to them, I said:
"Below is the host
of time immemorial,
and though I breath,
I crave to visit
for a short while."

Erictho What happened afterwards?

Laodamia I woke up.

Erictho It's clear you had some premonition of this visit.

Laodamia That's what I now know. *(pauses)* I can't live without Protesilaus.

Erictho There's a way you can remain with him.

Laodamia How? He has to stay and I have to leave.

Erictho You don't have to leave.

Laodamia Yes, I do: the living can't remain in the underworld. *(pauses)* Are you suggesting I kill myself?

Erictho You'll never be separated from him in death.

Laodamia This might come as a shock to you, but I already had thoughts of ending my life. My first suicidal impulse occurred upon discovery of my husband's death. If Hecate hadn't pulled the noose from my hands, you'd be speaking to my ghost now. My suicidal intentions returned after Persephone's refusal. You see - I'm no stranger to self-destruction.

Erictho I know. I also read thoughts, and I instantly saw these desires in you. Even now, as I look at you, I see the agony of solitariness. Protesilaus' death doesn't agonize you so much, as the thought of being left alone; you've never been alone in your life. You married at a very young age, and before marriage you lived with your family. You've never been faced with this situation.

Laodamia That's true.

Erictho You're already in the precincts of Hades, and if you kill yourself, you'll remain where you are.

Laodamia You're right. How can I end my life quickly and painlessly? I abhor violence.

Erictho I knew you'd ask; that's why I brought this box. I got it after I left your husband and the two goddesses. *(walks to the table, picks up the box, and gives it to Laodamia)*

Laodamia I didn't notice it before. What's so special about this box?

Erictho It's death.

Laodamia Is it some sort of poison?

Erictho No, it's a spirit's breath that lulls you into the darkness.

Laodamia All I have to do then is open the box.

Erictho And you'll find salvation.

Laodamia Won't you be affected?

Erictho Of course not. I'm immortal. *(gives her the box)* I give you the means, but you alone are death's instrument.

Laodamia takes the box, removes the cover, and instantly falls to the ground. Erictho stands before Laodamia and addresses her.

Erictho Sleep, sleep, Laodamia, sleep till there's no awakening. I bear you no grudge: your death is revenge against Hecate. When she discovers your corpse, she'll be humiliated and her desire to return to the underworld will be forever quenched. Hecate has always been my rival. Before I came here she was considered the greatest witch in the cosmos. It was unbearable for me to be second best, and so I thought of a plan to dispose of her. And what a brilliant plan it was. I began the rumour about Persephone and Hades and blamed it on Hecate, who then had to leave the underworld. You see, she suspected rightly. *(pauses)* The underworld needs only one witch and it is I. Let Hecate return to Mount Olympus; I'll stay here and retain my privileges of honour. Laodamia, did you see how easily I persuaded Persephone to change her mind? Soon she and Hecate will view the workings of a goddess unequaled, unrivaled.

PART SIX

Persephone and Hecate enter. They are shocked at seeing Laodamia lying on the ground, but quickly understand what has happened: they recognize the box that is still held in Laodamia's hands.

Hecate *(looking at the box)* What have you done, Erictho? I recognize that box and know what it does.

Persephone So do I. Why did you give it her?

Erictho Because she wanted to remain with her husband.

Hecate You shouldn't have satisfied her suicidal appetite.

Persephone *(touching Laodamia's pulse)* She's still alive. It hasn't yet killed her. Hecate, save her.

Erictho *(attempts to stop Hecate)* Let her be! She chose to die.

Persephone Stay away, Erictho. You've gone too far this time. I won't listen to you anymore. Hecate, hurry. Begin your spell.

Hecate *(kneels before Laodamia and takes hold of the box)*
Spirit of death,
I cast upon you a net
made not of intricate mesh
but of words
that are magnetic
and electrifying.
And I admonish you:
escape will bring no success,
but only piercing entanglement.
By the force of my hand,
I yank you out of this body
and send you to oblivion.

Hecate closes the lid. Laodamia slowly awakens.

Laodamia *(touching her arms)* Am I dead? That's strange; I still feel the same.

Hecate You're still alive. We saved you.

Laodamia Why? I don't want to leave.

Persephone You have no choice.

Laodamia Erictho gave me the box.

Hecate She shouldn't have. Erictho, it's one thing to battle me, but to harm her is beyond reproach. You're truly evil.

Persephone Erictho, I'll deal with you later. Laodamia,

you've been given a second chance. Consider yourself fortunate. You wanted me to restore your husband, but I restored you. Now leave the underworld and deal with your loss. I'm not suggesting you forget your husband - you can never do that - but resume living. Your grief has consumed you unnaturally.

Laodamia His death is difficult to accept.

Persephone Death is part of the human condition and you can't avoid it. Now leave. Your reason for being here is over.

Laodamia Hecate, I need your help. I don't remember how we got here. I'm afraid of getting lost.

Hecate Of course I'll escort you. I'm anxious to leave and return to my real home.

Persephone Hecate, by all means, escort Laodamia, but return here. I want you to come back. I promise, things have changed; I've changed. I want to renew our friendship.

Erictho What are you doing, Persephone? Let her stay on Mount Olympus. She has no place here anymore.

Persephone *(turning to Erictho rather angrily)* Don't meddle in: this doesn't concern you.

Erictho is taken aback; for the first time, she is fearful of Persephone, whose behaviour is unexpected and startling.

Persephone *(turning to Hecate)* Do you remember how inseparable we were? I consulted you in all matters.

Hecate Today I've learned that the past can't be relived. Erictho's right. My home isn't here anymore.

Persephone Is there no way I could convince you to return to your old home?

Hecate Nothing can change my mind. *(turning to Laodamia)* Laodamia, we better head off. A long, arduous journey awaits us. But I won't desert you once you reach home. I plan to spend some time with you, so you can get through these difficult times.

Laodamia You're a true friend, Hecate. It's too bad this journey turned out to be unpleasant for you, as it was for me. It's obvious you were never treated with respect. You're right to refuse Persephone.

Hecate I'll never let them humiliate me again. Look at how they treated you. Let's depart with dignity and self-respect. Unfortunately, you're required to make another visit, but for me it's a final farewell.

Hecate and Laodamia exit, while Persephone and Erictho remain on stage.

THE END

CHARACTERS

Stheneboea	Queen of Argos; wife of Proetus and daughter of Iobates, the king of Lycia
Merope	Wife of Bellerophon and sister of Stheneboea
Bellerophon	Slayer of the Chimaera and rider of Pegasus; husband of Merope
Clio	Servant of Stheneboea
Naya	Servant of Stheneboea

STHENEBOEA

PART ONE

Palace at Argos. It is in the wee hours of the morning. A woman sleeps on a chair, holding a letter in her hands. She is Stheneboea, the queen of Argos. Two other women enter the room. They are the queen's servants, and their names are Clio and Naya. The room is dark, dimly lit by candles. Clio and Naya address the audience.

Clio Eros always hovers about you like a bee,
ready to sting your heart and make it bleed.
You might not feel when he stings,
but when you are stung,
you feel a tingle
that quickly grows
into unbearable pain.
Stheneboea, sitting beside us,
was once stung by Eros,
her wound Bellerophon.

Naya Look at Stheneboea's hands,
and you will see a letter
that has brought her agony,
but we don't know why.
We think its subject is Bellerophon,
a name she has mumbled
all day and all night.
Sleep has come to her late
and now soothes her to our delight.

Clio Bellerophon once hovered about the Chimaera,
whose nose blazed with fire,
whose ears steamed with vapour,
and from whose mouth burst forth

	a spotted viper. But it took one moment for Bellerophon to extinguish the flame.
Naya	Pegasus, his flying companion, was born from evil. The blade swished, slashing the air, and snakes plummeted from Medusa's head. Pegasus then sprang from the gash, the Gorgon's blood slithering through his veins.
Clio	Time is a mirror, a reflection of appearances; it hides truth, which can be seen not with the eyes, but with the mind.
Naya	Memory is part of time and from it we reconstruct reality and the past.

Stheneboea awakens and starts speaking to Clio and Naya.

Stheneboea	*(rising from her chair)* I was sleeping so soundly and blissfully, but now I wake up distressed.
Clio	What's written in that letter? You refused to tell us last night. I thought we are your friends, not only your servants.
Stheneboea	*(lays the letter on the desk)* Very well. You'll soon know. Father sent this letter and writes that my sister got married a year ago.
Clio	That's wonderful. Is this why you were upset all night? You should be happy for Merope. Who's her husband?
Stheneboea	That's the source of my pain.
Clio	I don't understand.
Stheneboea	*(hesitatingly)* It's Bellerophon.

Clio You're still in love with him, aren't you?

Stheneboea Yes.

Clio And you're jealous, despite the fact you're married. I hope you won't wreck your sister's marriage.

Stheneboea I'd never hurt Merope. By the way, she and Bellerophon are arriving today and will be staying with us for a couple of days.

Clio Does Merope know about you and Bellerophon?

Stheneboea No, I never told her and I hope he didn't. She mustn't ever find out that I once tried to seduce him. Anyway, that was a long time ago and nothing happened between us. You know I was rejected.

Clio Yes, we do. How did Bellerophon end up in Lycia, your father's kingdom?

Stheneboea Because of me.

Clio How?

Stheneboea I am ashamed to say…

Clio Please tell us.

Stheneboea No, I can't.

Clio *(comes up to Stheneboea and caresses her)* We promise to keep it a secret.

Stheneboea *(hesitatingly)* All right, but you can't tell anyone, not my husband, not my sister, and least of all, not Bellerophon.

Clio & Naya *(together)* We promise.

Stheneboea I never told you what I did after Bellerophon turned me down. He was unemployed, and I suggested that he go work for my father, who was in need of mercenaries. Bellerophon took my advice, and before he left for Lycia, I wrote a letter to my father, accusing the hero of attempted seduction. I asked Dad to kill him.

Naya *(shocked)* Why did you do that?

Stheneboea *(loudly)* Because I was scorned, insulted! I had to punish that fool!

Naya *(raising her voice)* What you did was wrong. Bellerophon, at least, did the right thing.

Stheneboea Watch your tone of voice. I am still your queen.

Clio *(calmly)* Let's control our tempers. Stheneboea, your father obviously didn't kill Bellerophon. What happened after he arrived at Lycia?

Stheneboea Father writes that he wanted Bellerophon dead but was afraid of being called a murderer. He decided to send him on various missions in the hope he'd die in the process. The first of these labours was the Chimaera, which no man could slay until Bellerophon. Everyone knows how he easily hacked it down. The next labours were a series of wars. Contrary to Father's expectations, Bellerophon emerged victorious in all his battles and even began to be called a hero throughout Greece. Dad then believed that Bellerophon was the gods' favourite and under their constant protection. Instead of seeking his death, he made him marry Merope.

Naya Bellerophon almost lost his life because of you.

Stheneboea No. I made Bellerophon into a hero like Heracles.

Naya I now understand why Merope and Bellerophon mustn't ever find out what you did.

Stheneboea Father never told them and you've already promised to keep your mouths shut.

Clio & Naya Yes, we did.

Stheneboea Merope would hate me if she knew. But I'm afraid of Bellerophon: who knows how he'd react.

Naya I've heard he has an uncontrollable temper.

Clio And is ruthless and merciless on the battlefield. You don't want to be his enemy.

Naya Stheneboea, you know him. Is this true?

Stheneboea Doesn't sound like the Bellerophon I knew. He must have changed fighting wars and killing monsters. He was always so mysterious and difficult to read. I think it was his mysteriousness that first drew me to him. He was so quiet and polite when he stayed with us.

Clio Stheneboea, you have never talked much about that visit. Where did you proposition Bellerophon? Where was your husband, Proetus?

Kommos (lyric dialogue) begins.

Stheneboea Proetus was gone on business, as he is accustomed, and I was alone when Bellerophon came looking for accommodation.
How could I have refused a harmless and hungry beggar?
My marriage was about convenience, my father's convenience.
He saw a worthy alliance between himself and Proetus, the king of Argos.

Clio You have never known love in your marriage.

Stheneboea My heart was first stung when I saw Bellerophon.

Naya You speak of the power of Eros.

Stheneboea Bellerophon walks the air like Helios,
who daily mounts his chariot
and brings light to earth and sea.

Clio Your wound has never healed, and I'm afraid you'll try to seduce Bellerophon again. Eros makes people bold.

Stheneboea Though my heart and mind tug me to different directions, it's my mind that's in control.
I don't want to be refused a second time.

Naya How did you seduce him when he first came to the palace?

Stheneboea Love's venom drugged me to the task.
One day we were walking in the garden,
and heavy rain began falling from the sky.
We hid under a palm tree so we could keep dry, but here was my chance to fulfill secret desires.
I revealed my feelings, and instead of delight,
there was shock, dismay.
He called me a vile adulteress and threatened me with death.

Clio Weren't you afraid?

Stheneboea No. I didn't believe he'd harm me.
But I was rejected and wanted revenge.
I convinced Bellerophon to become my father's mercenary,
and as he whimpered away to Lycia,
I sent secret instructions to make him pay.
Bellerophon had no inkling of the labours awaiting him.

Naya You don't feel sorry for what you did.
The heroism of Bellerophon was born from

your scorn, and now his fame, like the sun,
scorches the land.
Is heroism innate or self-taught?
Can valour come from lies?
His marriage, which you abhor, also comes from your lies.

Stheneboea I couldn't attend their wedding,
a tent stretched out in the open field,
harbour from the heat.
Thousands droned to see the wedding of hero and princess.

Clio There's a deep jealousy of sisters in this family.
You have always claimed that Merope is more beautiful and more fortunate;
and yet this is untrue.
When will you stash away childhood rivalry?
She's a kind and loving sister.

Naya Remember the tale of Psyche,
who was urged by her sisters
to kill Eros, her winged husband.
This hastened their end.

Stheneboea I'm not like Psyche's sisters; I only wish Merope happiness and prosperity.
(Kommos ends. Someone knocks on the door.)
I think our guests have arrived.

PART TWO

The door opens and Merope enters. She runs up to Stheneboea and hugs her. Stheneboea is aloof.

Merope *(excitedly)* Hello, Stheneboea.

Stheneboea *(standoffish)* Merope.

Merope *(embraces Clio and Naya)* Clio and Naya, my dear friends.

Clio & Naya Welcome, Merope.

Stheneboea How was your trip?

Merope It was fine, but long. We did get to see beautiful scenery on the way. I'm so happy to be here. It's been too long. I think the last time we saw each other was a year ago, before my wedding.

Stheneboea Then you were single and now you're married. Bellerophon is lucky to have such a beautiful wife.

Merope You always flatter me. I wish Bellerophon would think the same as you do. *(pausing)* I just arrived. I shouldn't start complaining the moment I walk into your house.

Stheneboea You're not complaining. What's this about Bellerophon?

Merope I don't think he finds me attractive.

Stheneboea I'm sure he does.

Merope No, he doesn't. I don't think so since last week.

Stheneboea What happened last week?

Merope We just had dinner and were reclining on the couch. Bellerophon turned to me and asked, "Do you think you ate a lot tonight?" I said, "No, the usual." He then touched my stomach and said, "No, you ate a lot." I felt so inadequate!

Naya He's so insensitive!

Stheneboea *(turning to Naya with a somewhat harsh tone)* Bellerophon insensitive! What do you know? You never met him. *(turning to Merope with a calmer tone)* He was probably kidding. Don't take it to heart.

Merope *(unconvincingly)* Perhaps I overreacted. I shouldn't be upset, but you know, men nowadays want their women to be like models. *(pauses)* By the way, where's your husband?

Stheneboea He's out of town, as usual.

Merope That's too bad, Bellerophon and I looked forward to seeing him. Bellerophon will be disappointed.

Stheneboea Where is he? Didn't he come with you?

Merope Of course he did. He's outside harnessing the horses and getting help with the luggage. He has a hard time carrying things since his accident.

Stheneboea When did he have an accident?

Merope You don't know about it? I thought you knew. He fell off Pegasus.

Stheneboea When did this happen?

Merope Before our wedding. There was a storm, and the thunder and lightening frightened poor Pegasus. Bellerophon was thrown off. It's a miracle he survived, but he now suffers from severe back pain and has trouble walking.

Bellerophon enters limping. He glances uncomfortably at Stheneboea and turns away. Stheneboea cannot hide her excitement.

Stheneboea Hello, Bellerophon.

Bellerophon Hello, Stheneboea. It's been a while. *(turning to Merope)* Our luggage is being brought in. *(turning to Stheneboea)* Where's Proetus?

Stheneboea He's out of town on business. Merope and I were just talking about your accident. Are you getting better?

Bellerophon No, I live with daily pain. I'll be limping for the rest of my life.

Stheneboea Do you still ride Pegasus? Maybe you shouldn't. I think he's become a dangerous beast.

Bellerophon No, he isn't. He's a good horse. The storm made him go crazy. He has always been afraid of thunder and lightening.

Stheneboea Why did you fly out on bad weather?

Bellerophon I had no choice. Your father commanded and so I took off. Your father doesn't like to be questioned or disobeyed: when he commands you do as you're told.

Stheneboea You make him sound like a tyrant.

Bellerophon *(raising his voice)* Well, he is a tyrant and a very powerful one. Power has made your father arrogant; you can never question him. He knows he's the most powerful ruler in Greece. He has conquered countless nations and has never been defeated in battle; thousands are under his sway.

Stheneboea *(also raising her voice)* I'm offended by your remarks. Dad is not arrogant. I'm sure he had good reason to send you out in a storm.

Bellerophon *(irritated)* His good reason was to deliver weapons to one of his allies engaged in war. He never cared about my life or safety. He always had good reason to send me on some mission. That was before I got married. These missions were the labours of my life.

Stheneboea Were they dangerous?

Bellerophon Extremely. I overcame them because I wanted to live. Failure meant death.

Stheneboea Which mission was the most dangerous?

Bellerophon All were; and they were also senseless. Your father first sent me to kill the Chimaera. Why, you may ask, did he want the Chimaera destroyed? Because it posed a great danger to humanity? The Chimaera was a harmless creature that lived alone in the mountain. Your father wanted it killed for his own prestige, and I was chosen as its executioner. Do you know that I still have nightmares of what I did? It was sleeping so peacefully when I decapitated it. I'm known for this murderous feat!

Stheneboea Perhaps we don't fully understand why Dad wanted you to kill the Chimaera. But he was justified in sending you against the Amazons, who threatened the security of Lycia.

Bellerophon That's your father's propaganda. The Amazons were never hostile to the kingdom of Lycia, nor did they constitute the axis of evil. Your father simply wanted to expand his domain, like all kings. Most of the time, wars are waged for the glory of one. The Amazons didn't deserve to be slaughtered by the thousands.

Stheneboea You have the audacity to come to my home and criticize Daddy! He's not a tyrant. You're forgetting that he is your father-in-law and your king.

Bellerophon Yes, I'm forgetting that we live in times where it's forbidden to question the king and his policies. Doing so means imprisonment or death. Society has not advanced, but has retreated. We should live a society where we can question the king's decisions without punishment. Yet in your father's kingdom, we fear for our lives. Ask your sister, she'd agree with me.

Stheneboea *(turning to Merope)* Is this true, Merope?

Merope *(timidly)* Maybe.

Stheneboea *(angrily)* You're a fine example to your subjects! How will they trust the king, if his own daughter and her husband question his management of the state? Do you want a revolution and have father overthrown and killed? Both of you will also be killed.

Merope Don't accuse us of being disloyal. I've never been afraid to disagree with Father, and he has never minded. But I always voice my opinion privately, in the house, away from the public ear.

Bellerophon That's right.

Stheneboea *(still talking to Merope)* Of course Daddy doesn't mind you disagreeing with him: you're his favourite. Don't deny it. I now understand why Bellerophon is so subversive. Daddy has always been fonder of you; he'd never admit it, but I have always sensed it. He made you a lavish wedding, but what kind of wedding did he make for me? He loves your husband, but to mine he has always shown sparse interest.

Merope *(upset)* We only know how to quarrel, and not

how to converse. This has been the nature of our relationship since childhood. And it's always about me being Daddy's favourite. I can't believe you're saying that my wedding was more extravagant than yours. This is mere fiction. Besides, what would you know about my wedding? You weren't even there. What was your excuse? Let me remember, you were ill.

Stheneboea Yes, I was ill at the time. You don't believe me?

Merope Fine, you were ill; let's not argue about this. That's not the main issue. Stheneboea, you have never been slighted, nor shown less favour: Dad has always loved us both. I see there's no use trying to convince you; I never could and today will be no exception. Bellerophon, we're leaving. We're obviously not welcome here.

Naya Stheneboea, don't let them go. They just arrived.

Stheneboea I uttered words I shouldn't have. Forgive me, Merope. Please stay. I was rash and inconsiderate.

Merope We did travel for many days to see you. It would be a pity to leave after we just arrived. I forgive you, Sthenenboea, as I always do. We'll stay.

Stheneboea Bellerophon, will you stay?

Bellerophon Yes.

Stheneboea Then everything is resolved. Tonight we'll celebrate your arrival. I'll tell the cooks to prepare a special meal.

Merope I hope we won't bicker for the remainder of our

	visit.
Stheneboea	I'll make sure we won't. Merope, would you like to come to the kitchen and help me choose the dishes for tonight?
Merope	Yes, Stheneboea. Lead the way. Bellerophon, we'll return shortly.

Stheneboea and Merope depart. Bellerophon, Clio, and Naya remain.

PART THREE

Bellerophon	I wasn't looking forward to this visit. I don't believe that Stheneboea and Merope won't start quarreling again. *(pauses)* You and Naya are Sthenenboea's good friends; she must confide in you.
Clio	She does.
Bellerophon	Do you know what happened the last time I was here?
Clio	We do.
Bellerophon	I need to know if she ever told Merope about it.
Clio	No, she never did.
Bellerophon	Ah, she's ashamed, no doubt. I have to admit that I was very tempted when Stheneboea came onto me; she's a very attractive woman, you know, but I held back. I acted honourably. It would have been immoral to sleep with a married woman. This is why I feel uncomfortable and awkward around her.
Clio	She's probably uncomfortable around you.

Bellerophon	I shouldn't pay attention to her. We're only here for a couple of days.

Bellerophon walks round the table and sees Stheneboea's letter. He picks it up. Clio and Naya become nervous.

Naya	That's Stheneboea's. Leave it alone.
Bellerophon	Why? Where is it from?
Naya	It's from Iobates, her father. Don't be nosy.
Bellerophon	If it's from Iobates, then it's my business to read it; he's my father-in-law, and I am heir to the throne. *(puts down the letter)* Perhaps you're right. It doesn't concern me. *(pauses)* Maybe it does. I'll read it. I don't trust Iobates; he and Stheneboea might want me to do some work for them. I need to find out what's in store for me.
Naya	Don't worry. No new hardships await you.
Bellerophon	How do you know? Did you read the letter?
Naya	No. I just know.

Naya tries to grab the letter from him, but he pulls it away. He starts reading it and becomes enraged.

Bellerophon	*(lays the letter on the desk)* Iobates says that I once tried to seduce Stheneboea and that's why he tried to have me killed. What does this all mean?
Naya	*(hesitatingly)* We don't know.
Bellerophon	You lie. *(violently grabs hold of her)*
Clio	Let go of her, you brute. Don't hurt her. Are you always violent with women?
Bellerophon	*(releases Naya)* Where did Iobates get this

preposterous idea? Is this what she told him?

Clio Yes.

Bellerophon Why?

Clio Because you refused to sleep with her. That was her revenge.

Bellerophon I did the right thing and I was punished for it. I now understand why Iobates put me through such misery: he believed his daughter and expected me to die in every mission. I always wanted to punish him, but now I see it's Stheneboea who really deserves to be punished.

Clio Don't you dare harm her. Try to forgive her. She was hurt when you turned her down; and when you're hurt you say things you don't really mean. She's still in love with you.

Bellerophon Is this true?

Clio Yes. That 's why you should forgive her. Keep in mind that revenge accomplishes nothing.

Bellerophon If I confront Stheneboea and accuse her of what she did, she'd deny everything and we'd start quarrelling. I don't want that; and I also don't want Merope to get hurt.

Clio Now you're talking sensibly. Think with your head and not with your heart. You learned too much today. Naya, let's get to work.

Naya We'll see you at dinner, Bellerophon.

Clio and Naya depart. Bellerophon sits on the chair and picks up the letter again.

Bellerophon Is there no justice in this world? Are the good always punished and the wicked rewarded? Stheneboea punished me because I refused to sleep with her. "She was hurt." That doesn't justify what she did to me. I never wanted to be a hero and fight monsters. She made my life a living hell, no doubt about it, and there isn't a day I don't feel guilt for those I have slain in battle. I had normal a life before I met Stheneboea. *(stands up)* I'm called a hero and I'll act as one. I've always felt helpless, but now I'll take charge. Stheneboea and Iobates will die tonight! Murder will reign in Argos and Lycia! Let me think, how will I kill Stheneboea? *(pauses)* I know. Love will be her undoing. I know from Clio and Naya that she still loves me. In the middle of the night I'll wake up Stheneboea and tell her I'm in love with her. She won't believe me, but I'll convince her; it's easy to persuade the one who loves you. She'll melt once she knows I want to marry her and take her away from this dismal life. We'll make our escape on Pegasus and once we're above land, I'll throw her off; that will be her end. I'll then fly to Lycia where I'll murder Iobates in his sleep. After that I'll escape to Asia where I can't be tracked or found. Stheneboea made me and for that she'll be rewarded!

Bellerophon departs. The stage is left empty. After a few moments Clio and Naya enter.

PART FOUR

Choral ode begins.

Clio A hero doesn't know who he is
and thinks he is constructed
by reputation and expectation,
but he is really made
of his imagination.
I fear Bellerophon's violence.
Will he harm Stheneboea?
It's hard to trust someone who has been
death's instrument.

Naya I pity the Chimaera,
a gentle creature,
harmless unless provoked;
in summertime it napped on the grass,
while birds scampered around its feet.
But it could not prophecy its doom.
I also pity the Amazons,
who are now extinct,
a unique race once thriving.
Heroism should not be born from destruction.

Clio Bellerophon's life is like a ship,
steered by rushing winds upon the violent sea
and drawn into whirlpools that swallow water.
Bellerophon is weary.
Survival compelled victory
wherever there was clanging of shields
on foreign fields.
His limp comes from the king's ludicrous commands.

Naya Voracious battle gnaws the spirit

and devours all,
coward and brave alike.
Don't be astonished when you see a stout man tumbling
and splintering his spear.
What makes a hero?
Bravery, strength?
Or is it trials and tribulations?
Does every hero need
Twelve Labours?

Clio He hides his scars from sight,
scars that goad his body and soul.
Does suffering bring wisdom,
as Aeschylus once said?
No.
Suffering brings cowering terror and delusions
which are invisible to all
except the one egged on.
All seek heroism, but is it worth
such a cost?

Naya Lycia surpasses all other lands
in arts, crafts, and wisdom,
and is ruled by Iobates,
the most powerful man in Greece.
What did Bellerophon mean?
Is the superpower led astray
by senselessness,
selfishness?

Clio Without government there's anarchy.
Let a new leader be spotted from the crowd,
one who can govern not by pride,
but by wisdom.
Kings sway the sceptre by their whims

and make a friend an enemy.

Naya I admire Merope, who is kind and loving.
Her happiness is her husband and two sons.
May she never know her sister's treachery.
Eros, you chose an unsuitable prey,
a married woman, whose heart pulsates
for another man.
Is it your custom to instill forbidden desire
and never let wounds heal?

Choral ode ends

Clio Dinner was quite tense, wasn't it?

Naya Yes, it was. Bellerophon and Stheneboea were very quiet, but Merope tried to enliven the conversation.

Clio Merope adores Bellerophon and looks at him like he's a god. But he doesn't treat her well; you could tell by the way he talks to her. She deserves better.

Naya I'm afraid for Stheneboea. I don't really trust Bellerophon. We need to make sure that she's never left alone with him.

Clio We'll be on our guard the next few days. Tonight we don't have to worry. They are all asleep by now. We should also go to bed. Good night, Naya.

Naya Good night.

Clio and Naya depart. After a few moments Bellerophon and Stheneboea enter.

PART FIVE

Stheneboea Why did you knock on my door and get me out of bed?

Bellerophon I couldn't sleep. I wanted to talk to you.

Stheneboea Couldn't it wait till morning?

Bellerophon No.

Stheneboea Did you enjoy dinner?

Bellerophon Yes, it was quite sumptuous.

Stheneboea You were silent the whole time. You seem uncomfortable being here.

Bellerophon Of course I am, considering my last visit.

Stheneboea Are you happy?

Bellerophon With Merope?

Stheneboea *(nods)*

Bellerophon I guess I am.

Stheneboea She's very happy, the happiest I've ever seen her.

Bellerophon We live well together.

Stheneboea Did you ever tell Merope about you and me?

Bellerophon No, that would devastate her and destroy whatever relationship you have with her.

Stheneboea You're right. You're her first love.

Bellerophon I know and I can say I'm also your first love.

Stheneboea You really flatter yourself. I love my husband.

Bellerophon You've never loved Proetus.

Stheneboea How would you know? This is the second time you've been to my house, and you think you know everything about me and my marriage.

Bellerophon I know you've always loved me.

Stheneboea Is this why you woke me up and got me out of bed? Just to mock me and make yourself feel desirable?

Bellerophon You don't have to be ashamed of your feelings for me.

Stheneboea I'm not ashamed of anything. Even if I loved you, that wouldn't change my situation. I have a husband.

Bellerophon Stheneboea, I'm unhappy. I lied before. I don't love Merope.

Stheneboea Poor Merope. Why did you marry her?

Bellerophon I had to. Your father pressured me.

Stheneboea Why are you telling me this?

Bellerophon Because... I love you. I have always loved you.

Stheneboea I don't believe you.

Bellerophon It's true.

Stheneboea You lie.

Stheneboea distances herself from Bellerophon. In the meantime Merope approaches the door, but stops; she is shocked by what she has just heard and remains frozen, unseen by Stheneboea and Bellerophon.

Bellerophon I love you, Stheneboea. There hasn't been a day I haven't thought about you.

Stheneboea What you're doing is dangerous, playing with my emotions.

Bellerophon I'm not toying with you, Stheneboea. Let's escape. All we have to do is hop on Pegasus and fly off. We'll fly far away where we can't be found. What about Asia? Pegasus could fly us there overnight. We could pick any Greek city along the coast and settle there. We'll get married and start our own family.

Stheneboea Let me recall your last visit. I wanted to go to bed with you, and you said no. Now you say you love me and want to run away with me.

Bellerophon I was so tempted when you came onto me. I immediately saw us in the act, but held back from fear. I didn't want to get caught by your husband; he would have killed me. But let me tell you that I wanted you then and I want you now.

Stheneboea You want to betray your wife.

Bellerophon You then wanted to betray your husband.

Stheneboea That's different.

Bellerophon How is it different? It's the same; we both have adulterous intentions. Stheneboea, we're on earth for one brief moment and don't know when we'll go. What are human beings? Just like flies. I know I should think of Merope and you should think of Proetus, but let us consider: are these the people we really want to be with the rest of our lives? I don't think so. I've already made up my mind: I prefer to be with you. Now it's up to you to decide; you can hop on Pegasus and leave with me or stay with your husband.

Stheneboea looks at Bellerophon and suddenly runs up to him. They embrace and kiss.

Stheneboea Let's leave tonight. We can't delay. Do we need any food or water for the journey?

Bellerophon Yes, we actually do. I'll get the supplies. Is there a way to the stable without being seen?

Stheneboea Go through that door. *(pointing at another door that has not yet been used)* No one will see you.

Bellerophon I'll go ahead and get things ready. I'll meet you there.

He departs by the door leading to the stable. Merope is still standing at the other door.

Stheneboea What should I make of Bellerophon? I rejoice, and yet I fear. Is he deceiving me? No, he can't be. *(pauses)* I am a married woman and a queen. What will people say about me if escape with him? That I am like Helen, who abandoned Menelaus and caused a great war? *(pauses)* No. I'm not like Helen, nor will any war be fought over me. My husband won't even notice me gone. Besides, Bellerophon is not a coward like Paris. He's a real hero. What about Merope? How can I betray her? She and Bellerophon have twin sons. *(pauses)* Bellerophon truly loves me and I feel the same for him. How can I say no? I've decided: Pegasus will soon whisk us away to a new life together.

Stheneboea departs by the door Bellerophon exited. Merope slowly enters the room and sits on a chair. Sullen, she stares down at the floor. After a few moments Clio and Naya enter.

PART SIX

Clio Merope, why are you up and not asleep? You look so sad and pale.

Merope *(quietly)* My world has crumbled.

Clio Why has your world crumbled?

Merope Bellerophon has betrayed me, and so has Stheneboea.

Clio When did this happen?

Merope Just now, a few moments ago.

Clio Tell us exactly what happened.

Merope I woke up and didn't find Bellerophon in bed. I went to look for him and found him with Stheneboea. They're in love! I hid behind the door and heard everything. They're probably gone by now, making their escape on Pegasus. I'm devastated.

Naya This makes no sense.

Merope It makes sense to me. I was there.

Naya Don't believe what you heard. Bellerophon deceived you and Stheneboea; he doesn't really love her.

Merope Why not?

Naya Because he blames her for all his suffering and probably wants to harm her.

Merope I don't understand what you're talking about. All I know is that they've always been in love and now have fled together. What am I going to tell my twin sons? That their father has abandoned them? They're so young. Stheneboea has always been jealous of me and couldn't bear my happiness; that's why she stole my husband. I was hoping our relationship

	would be mended in this visit, but I see that there can be no mending. I hate her.

Suddenly the door flings open and Bellerophon enters holding Stheneboea, who can barely walk. He seats her on a chair. She seems to be in immense pain.

Merope	*(turning to Bellerophon)* Why have you returned? Weren't you supposed to be somewhere in Asia by now? I heard everything.
Naya	What's wrong with you, Stheneboea? What did he do to you?
Bellerophon	I tossed her off Pegasus while we were in the air. A tree broke her fall. I couldn't leave her there to die.
Naya	You show remorse after doing the deed.
Merope	There is no man on earth as base as you, Bellerophon; you're a craftsman of deception. Naya was right. You don't love her and I don't think you ever loved me. You just love yourself. Why did you do this to my sister?
Bellerophon	I'll tell you why. She told your father that I tried to seduce her the last time I was here; that's why he kept sending me on these horrific labours.
Merope	Didn't he want you to become a hero?
Bellerophon	No, he wanted me dead. It's all because of her, her lies. So I punished her.
Stheneboea	*(muttering)* I'm in so much pain. Merope.

Naya, Clio, and Merope run to Stheneboea.

Merope	I'm here, Stheneboea.
Stheneboea	Will you ever forgive me?

Merope I'm in shock. I don't know if I can ever forgive you or Bellerophon. But I don't want you to die. We need a doctor. Clio, Naya, go get help.

Stheneboea *(looking at Clio and Naya)* Don't go. I'm beyond saving. *(pauses)* Where's Bellerophon?

Bellerophon I'm right here.

Stheneboea Bellerophon, do you remember when we hid under the palm tree and the rain was pouring down?

Bellerophon Yes.

Stheneboea There I revealed my innermost desires.

Bellerophon That palm tree was no refuge from the storm, but its beginning.

Stheneboea I forgive you, Bellerophon.

Bellerophon Why? I sent you to your death.

Stheneboea I still forgive you.

Bellerophon What have I done? How can I ever live with myself?

Stheneboea gasps and dies.

Merope *(shaking her)* Stheneboea, Stheneboea!

Bellerophon and Merope remain motionless around Stheneboea. Clio and Naya turn to the audience.

Clio Revenge is a shadow
through which you can pass your hand
and feel nothing.
Bellerophon sought revenge but couldn't find it;
what he did find was guilt,
the torture of his soul.

Naya
He was known as the slayer of the Chimaera,
but now he'll be known as the slayer of
Stheneboea.
I pity Merope,
who feels
grief and betrayal.
Bellerophon has pierced her heart
and trust.

Clio
If you look into the windows of this house,
you will see a queen
annihilated by love.
Bellerophon for her was a light
upon a tower
offering salvation to ships
in the foggy sea;
but he smashed her ship upon the jutting rocks.

Naya
The mind is a dense forest
in which it's difficult to see
the wind, the sun,
insects crawling on trees,
and bees gathering pollen
from every flower.
In this forest beware the bee,
whose sting dazzles the senses
and loosens the wits.

THE END

ῥεῖ δὲ γάλακτι πέδον, ῥεῖ δ' οἴνῳ,
ῥεῖ δὲ μελισσᾶν νέκταρι.

The ground flows with milk; it flows with wine;
it flows with the nectar of bees.

EURIPIDES *BACCHAE* 143-4

σὺν δ' ἀλαθείᾳ βαλῶν
καὶ μελιγλώσσου τις ὑμνήσει χάριν
Κηΐας ἀηδόνος.

People will acquire truth
when they sing of the charming, honey-tongued
nightingale from Keos.

BACCHYLIDES ODE 3. 96-8